A Seasonal Journal

with Pleasures, Plans,
and Projects for
Home and Garden

Watercolors and Notes by
Lauren Jarrett

Harry N. Abrams, Inc., Publishers, New York

Effort, attention to detail, and love are
what count in cooking, art, and life.

There are endless sources, remembered, recognized, and not, that
all contribute to the look, sense, and feel of my watercolors and the
seasonal notes that accompany them. With grateful acknowledg-
ment of help and inspiration—to Ruth Peltason, my editor at
Abrams, who pushes and pulls, suggests and questions, adds and
subtracts, until at last a shape appears and seems to affirm itself; to
John Perkins, who taught me the nuts and bolts of gardening; to the
Nature Conservancy, which contributes immeasurably to my life;
and lastly, my thanks to the long line of grandmothers, fairy god-
mothers, mothers, mentors, sisters, and friends from whom one
learns.

Editor: Ruth A. Peltason
Designer: Bob McKee

Preceding page: Black Iris

ISBN 0-8109-7638-2
Copyright © 1987 Lauren Jarrett
Published in 1987 by Harry N. Abrams, Incorporated, New York
Times Mirror Books
Printed and bound in Japan

Introduction

I grew up surrounded by the arts of gardening, cooking, and living. Nature and art have always seemed interrelated to me and have combined to form the central theme in my life.

My grandparents lived on a small farm outside New York City, where I spent much of my childhood. My grandfather was an art director, painter, naturalist, linguist, traveler, hiker, and farmer. My grandparents' farmhouse was a treasure trove for a young girl, particularly my grandfather's studio into which I was occasionally allowed. The quiet magic of the place, the orderliness of his collections, and the detail in his work quite captivated me. My grandparents raised goats and chickens and had a huge garden filled with vegetables and flowers. My grandmother taught me to garden and to cook, to arrange flowers, and to know the birds that filled the yard. More tolerant than most, she would let me raid her new crop of peas or her raspberry bushes, and show me how to remove raspberry stains from my dress to avoid a scolding. There was always a cookie jar in the corner of her kitchen, filled with her spice cookies. My jobs were to feed the chickens and to collect the eggs. Each summer I had baby goats as pets; they romped with me like puppies and slept on my lap when I would sit on the front porch swing. My grandfather took me to the woods and taught me the names for things—he knew every flower, tree, bird, and rock. Learning names was a way to become acquainted with the wealth and variety in nature and to begin looking at details more closely. Along with the names I heard flower and animal fables, Indian legends, woodland fairy tales, and nature lore. A strong sense of kinship with nature came from that early combination of lore, legend, and a growing awareness of the natural world.

My mother indulged and encouraged my collecting, planned field trips, helped with plant identification, and allowed me more drawer space for butterflies, shells, rocks, skulls, feathers, and pressed flowers than for clothes. I thanked her by arranging everything she had, from pots and pans to salads, fruit platters, and cold buffets, all in painstaking bundles or intricate patterns, usually more lovely and interesting than practical. As a child the finding, sorting, naming, and arranging of things always seemed magical to me, and I worked at my collections in accordance with that feeling. When I began painting, objects found at the beach, in the woods, along stream banks, in family attics, at flea markets, toy stores, and museum shops seemed to combine well for me in my watercolors with the magic that I remembered from my childhood.

My winter refuge during college was the floriculture greenhouse complex. There were sections of tropical plants, orchards, cacti, cultivated flowers, and hydroponic experiments, each with a different smell, temperature, and humidity. I drew flowers in the warm, moist air while other art students drew from a model in drafty studios. When spring came, I moved outside to the perennial beds or over to the agricultural school's barns to draw or just play with the lambs, calves, and piglets. Later, I worked in a greenhouse and learned more of the gardener's skills while borrowing orchids to draw. The drawings led me to my first jobs as a book illustrator. Drawing and painting for cookbooks and gardening books bring together my real loves and skills. But it is a deep appreciation of nature and the domestic arts that fills my life and directs my efforts.

Out on the South Fork of Long Island, my life is full of seasonal pleasures—whether they are grown and harvested, cooked, painted, or just observed and enjoyed. Each contributes to a life that is close to nature and the patterns of the year. I've organized the journal to provide hints, tips, and suggestions in a seasonal progression, much as I would use them—the reminders and notes on houseplants, cut flowers, and holiday plants will guide you through a year full of flowers. . . seasonal recipes and menu ideas appear throughout, household tips are handy any time. As well, the spring, summer, and autumn spreads are mixtures of helpful how-to information, country lore, and a bit of whimsy. Monthly notes and reminders will give you a head start on seasonal chores and planning, no matter where you live—and feel free to write in your own notes and reminders. But mostly, experience the joys of the year and the ways they are reflected in the arts of living.

Lauren Jarrett
East Hampton

Jacqueline's Birthday Flowers

Lauren Jarrett

January

RESOLUTIONS — IF YOU HAVEN'T
MADE ANY

Lose weight
Firm up
Catch up
Slow down
Learn something
Take a class
Take a risk
Start a journal
Write a book
Laugh more
Hug more
Look harder
Listen better
Learn to love
Live every day

2

3

4

5

6

7

Jacqueline's Birthday Flowers

9

10

11

12

13

14

LAUREN'S MUFFINS FOR A WINTER
BREAKFAST OR EXPEDITION

Soak 1 c bran in 1 c buttermilk for 5
minutes. Cream together 3 TB melted
butter, 1 beaten egg, and 1/3 c maple
syrup. Add to bran and buttermilk.
Mix 1 c whole wheat flour, 1/2 c
rolled oats, 2 tsp baking powder, 1 tsp
baking soda, and 1/4 tsp salt. Add to
bran mixture. Add 3/4 c chopped
walnuts. Fold in 1 1/2 c frozen
raspberries, blackberries, or
blueberries. Pour into well-buttered
tins or cups and bake in a preheated
375° oven for 30 minutes. Makes
10–12 large muffins

French Roof in Snow

CYCLAMEN (*CYCLAMEN PERSICUM*)

Energy-conscious households are best for cyclamens—keep yours blooming all winter long by watering regularly but judiciously and by finding them a nice cool spot away from strong sunlight or dry heat. After their long flowering season, allow cyclamens to dry out and die back; then place them in a cool room until new growth appears. Later, repot them and keep relatively warm while the new leaves are developing; afterward, return cyclamens to a cooler spot.

16

17

18

19

20

21

Cyclamen and Dragon

23

24

25

26

27

28

HOUSEHOLD TIPS

🐛 Glassware is strengthened by slow-boiling in lightly salted water.

🐛 Hairline cracks in china can be concealed by boiling gently in milk for 1 hour.

🐛 Clean aluminum by boiling it with apple pairings.

🐛 To remove stains from a whole set of flatware, place it in a pan and cover with sour milk overnight. Then rinse the flatware in cold water and again in hot water and wipe dry.

🐛 To clean silver without endless polishing, put it in an aluminum pan or a bucket with a piece of aluminum foil. Add water and laundry detergent and soak for 15 minutes. Rinse and wipe dry.

🐛 Silverware tarnished with egg can be cleaned by rubbing it with damp salt, then rinsed and wiped dry.

🐛 To season a skillet or iron casserole, lightly grease and bake it at 450° for 30 minutes. When it has cooled, scour it with fine steel wool, wash with soap, rinse, and dry.

🐛 For Pets: You can remove pet fur and hair from upholstery and clothes by dampening a sponge or your hand and passing it lightly over the furry surface.

🐛 Try club soda to flush out a pet stain or try soaking the stain with hydrogen peroxide and a drop of ammonia for 15 minutes. You can also spread salt on a pet-stained carpet spot, wet with water to make a thick paste, let set for 1 day, and vacuum it up.

Chaise from France

NOTES & REMINDERS FOR FEBRUARY

Attend to your resolutions.
Plan for Valentine's Day.
Send for seed catalogues if you haven't already.
Plant early flower seeds inside.
Take cuttings from wintered-over plants.
Force stems of apple, crab apple, forsythia, daphne,
    pear, pussy willow, quince, spirea, and witch
    hazel for a midwinter burst of bloom.

Resume houseplant fertilizer at $\frac{1}{2}$ strength.
Check, sharpen, repair, and replace garden tools.
Start an exercise program.
Learn to knit.
Make a fire to read by.
Put all your photographs in albums.
Write a book.
Vacation in a warm place.

MORE NOTES:

Seed Packet Arrangement

1

2 Groundhog Day

3

4

LOVE POTIONS AND LORE

- Think of the one you love while swallowing a four-leaf clover; your love will be returned.
- Hard-boil an egg, cut it in half, discard the yolk, and fill the halves with salt. Sit on something you have never sat on before, eat the egg, and walk to bed backward; you will dream of your future mate.
- Cut a lemon in half, rub both pieces on the four corners of your bed, and sleep with the lemon halves under your pillow. If you see your lover in a dream, he or she will be faithful; if not, he or she will be unfaithful.
- Peel an apple without breaking the skin, swing the peel around your head three times, then throw it over your shoulder. When it lands, it will form the initial of your lover.

5

6

7

Still Life with Morning Glories and Geese

TULIP TIP

Tulips are greedy drinkers and must be rationed, lest they overdo and fall over limp in the process. Cut tulips only need to be in a little water—give them an inch of water at a time and they will remain standing straight on firm stems.

MORE LOVE POTIONS AND LORE

- ❦ Boil red and white rose petals in 385 drops of water for one-sixteenth of an hour. Add three drops to your lover's drink.
- ❦ Offer your lover a double-chocolate fudge sundae. Chocolate is rich in a substance related to amphetamines, which may account for the erratic behavior of people in love.

9

10

11

Abraham Lincoln's Birthday 12

13

St. Valentine's Day 14

Tulips, Balloons, and Parasols

15

16

17

RESORT VACATION CHECKLIST

At this time of the year your beach-necessity memory has dimmed; don't forget to pack:

Cool cottons
Sweats for evening strolls
A light jacket
Sunglasses
Sun hat, straw hat, and scarves
Suntan oils and sunblocks
Your smallest bathing suit
Lotions for après sun
Lots of books
A bag for shell collecting
Camera equipment
A sketchbook or journal

18

19

20

21

Pink Wall with Vine

February

ORCHIDS

Greenhouses, especially tropical ones filled with orchids, are wonderful refuges from winter's unending cold. Even without a greenhouse, orchids are easy enough to grow and enjoy. Orchids have been collected since the 17th century and cultivated since the 19th century; there are about 25,000 species and 50,000 orchid hybrids. They are characterized by thick, fleshy, food storage parts called pseudobulbs and by flowers with three sepals and three petals; one petal is always modified, often larger, and differently colored. Orchids need warmth, humidity, and light. Tropical areas native to orchids have 10–14 hours of sunlight which should be approximated at home with additional artificial light. Daytime temperatures should be 68–70 degrees and nighttime temperatures 60–64 degrees. Adequate humidity is best achieved by putting orchids on a tray of wet gravel above a heat source. Keep them away from draughts. Water orchids sparingly with room-temperature water and feed them only in the summer. Remove dead leaves and stake plants for support. Pot orchids in orchid mixture, usually shredded fir bark, osmunda fiber, and sphagnum moss.

23

24

25

26

27

28

Orchid Assortment

February

NOTES & REMINDERS FOR MARCH

Plan for the First of Spring and Easter.
Repot houseplants and resume full strength
  fertilizer.
Start vegetable seeds inside.
Thin and transplant February's seedlings.
Force daffodils for Easter.
Begin work in the garden.
Uncover perennials and shrubs.
Fertilize and lime the yard.

Thin and prune raspberries, blackberries,
  blueberries, and grapes.
Plant peas, radishes, spinach, lettuce, and onions
  outside.
Begin Easter baskets.
Color some eggs.
Take up running or brisk walking.
Go fly a kite.

MORE NOTES:

_____

_____

_____

_____

_____

_____

_____

_____

_____

_____

_____

_____

_____

_____

Seed Can and Wild Flowers

1

WHOLE WHEAT-GRAIN BREAD

When March winds inevitably blow winter back into your life, it's a good time to bake bread. Bread baking is an almost foolproof venture that warms you while you're making it, warms the kitchen while it's baking, and warms everybody while it's eaten.

Scald 2½ c milk to just below the boiling point; set in cold water until lukewarm, then stir in 6 TB honey and ¼ c oil. Dissolve 1 TB dry yeast in ¼ c warm water and add to the milk when it is lukewarm. Stir in 2 c white flour and 2 c whole wheat flour, beat the thick batter 100 times with a wooden spoon, and let it rise in a warm place for about 1 hour.

Add 2 TB salt, 1 c rolled oats, 1 c bran, and 2 c whole wheat or white flour until dough comes away from the sides of the bowl. Turn out on a floured board and knead for 15 minutes or until the dough is smooth. Let the dough rise for 50 minutes or until it has doubled in bulk, then punch it down, and let rise for another 40 minutes.   Form 2 loaves, place them in oiled bread pans, let the loaves rise for 20 minutes, and bake in a preheated 350° oven for 1 hour. The smell of baking bread will make it hard to wait until it cools, but it does slice more easily, if that matters. Makes 2 loaves

9

10

11

DANDELION (*TARAXACUM OFFICINALE*)

Pick the first dandelion you see and hurry it off to a friend, or tuck it into a buttonhole. The sunny yellow head of a dandelion announces the arrival of spring. Dandelion, or *dents de lion*, French for lion's tooth, is a golden treat for some and a weed for others, but its high content of vitamins A & C make it a fine spring tonic for those who would gather the young leaves for tea or wine-making. The leaves can be boiled like spinach or mixed with lamb's quarters for an early wild salad. Once the summer's heat has turned the leaves bitter, try wishing on the puffy seed heads instead. If they all come off on the first blow, your wish will come true.

BUTTERCUP (*RANUNCULUS FASCICULARIS*)
Hold a buttercup under someone's chin—a butter lover's chin will reflect the yellow color.

12

13

14

Holstein Sign

M arch

PASTA PRIMAVERA WITH SCALLOPS
AND SHRIMP FOR THE FIRST OF
SPRING

*Celebrate the vernal equinox and the
return of spring with flowers and this
fresh-tasting combination of seafood
and vegetables over pasta.*

Simmer ½ lb scallops and 1 lb shelled
shrimp in 1 c *each* water and white
wine. Save the broth. Cut into bite-
size pieces ½ to 1 cup *each*: broccoli,
beans, snow peas, zucchini, celery, red
pepper, and mushrooms. Steam all but
mushrooms and red pepper until just
done. Sauté 1 clove chopped garlic, 3
shallots, mushrooms, and red pepper
in olive oil. Combine 4 TB melted
butter, 1 c seafood broth, ½ c cream,
and grated Parmesan cheese to taste in
a pan. Toss with the vegetables,
seafood, and sautéed mushrooms.
Adjust seasonings. Combine with 1 lb
pasta, garnish with parsley and
Parmesan, and serve with a spring
salad and Pouilly Fuissé. Serves 4

16

St. Patrick's Day 17

18

19

20

21

Still Life with Plum Jar, Apricots, and Shells

22

23

24

25

26

27

28

STAINS—LIFE IS FULL OF THEM

❦ My grandmother taught me to use boiling water on raspberry stains (stolen berries) and cold water on blood stains (scratches and cuts).

❦ For fruit stains, you can also try a little bleach with hot water; rinse.

❦ Blood and meat juice stains need cold water and soap or club soda and cold water.

❦ For egg, cream, or milk stains, use cold water and mild soap; rinse.

❦ Treat coffee or tea stains similarly, then use hot water.

❦ For chocolate stains, follow cold water and soap with borax or bleach and cold water; rinse.

❦ For grease and oil, use warm water and soap or try a little turpentine, or wet the spot with hydrogen peroxide and 1 drop of ammonia; rinse thoroughly.

❦ For mildew, use cold water and lemon juice or bleach, and rinse.

❦ Soak perspiration stains for 30 minutes in 1 qt warm water, $\frac{1}{2}$ tsp liquid dish-washing detergent, and 1 TB ammonia; rinse and soak again for 1 hour in 1 qt warm water and 1 TB vinegar. Rinse.

❦ For makeup stains, use wet-spot remover and a few drops of ammonia; rinse.

❦ For water-based paint, use warm water and soap; for oil-based paint, use turpentine or 70% isopropyl alcohol, then warm water and soap; rinse.

❦ Grass stains should soak in cold water and soap; try turpentine or 70% isopropyl alcohol and rinse thoroughly.

❦ Wax should be scraped off; then use a warm iron and absorbent paper to remove the rest; for a residue, try 70% isopropyl alcohol and then a little bleach; rinse.

❦ Clean suede by rubbing it with a piece of stale bread.

30

31

NOTES & REMINDERS FOR APRIL

Plan for Easter.
Finish Easter baskets and egg coloring.
Take cuttings from geraniums, coleus, fuchsia, and impatiens.
Start herbs and tender vegetables from seed inside.
Set out hardy vegetable seedlings (broccoli, cabbage, cauliflower).
Divide perennials.
Plant roses and strawberries.
Plant trees and shrubs.

Take sports and yard equipment out of the garage or shed.
Change storms and screens.
Clean porch or patio.
Paint something in your house or outside to freshen it for spring.
Go to yard sales.
Make a spring picnic.
Take a hike.
Climb a tree.

MORE NOTES:

_____

_____

_____

_____

_____

South Fork Suffolks

Spring

Once winter has loosened its grip, your houseplants will need attention in the spring after their long dormant season.

Fill a window box or planter with begonias, coleus, dusty miller, geraniums, impatiens, petunias, and periwinkle (vinca) trailing over the edge. Or plant a container of lettuce or herbs.

Flowers with the prefix "lady" have protective qualities, and are thought to honor the Virgin Mary, although their earlier allegiance was to one of the earth goddesses.

Divide and replant late summer and fall flowering perennials in the spring. Plant shallow, fibrous-rooted perennials such as asters, bell-flowers, carnations, chrysanthemums, coral bells, pinks, shasta daisies, and veronicas.

Put soap under your nails before gardening for an easy cleanup.

An annual grows, flowers, and seeds in one season; usually tender, it is killed by frost.

A perennial lives from year to year; the top dies down, but the roots live through the winter.

Tender plants which are susceptible to frost must be set out when the soil is warm—tomatoes, corn, basil, melon, and impatiens.

Hardy plants can withstand winter's cold, but this is a relative term depending on the specific temperature zone.

Repotting

1. Remove plant from old pot.
2. Trim old roots; loosen soil, and repot.

Dividing Perennials

1. Use two forks to separate the plants.
2. Cut through the roots with a knife.

Hanging Basket

1. Line a basket with sphagnum moss.
2. Fill basket with potting soil. Arrange and set plants; slant trailing plants toward the edge.

Cuttings

1. Plants with runners need only a small pot and a hairpin clip to produce a new plant.

2. Stem cuttings should be 3–5 inches long; cut just below a leaf notch on the stem.

3. Trim the bottom leaves, then put the stem in sand or vermiculite to root. Root hormone powder is helpful. A leaf cutting is rooted similarly; plantlets will form at the base of the leaf.

4. To make a leaf vein cutting, make small cuts across the leaf's veins, put the leaf right side up on moist sand, secure with hairpins. Cover with a plastic bag. Transplant when roots have formed.

Plan a garden with respect to the character of the site and the style of the surroundings: put a formal arrangement or a wild border in a similar landscape. Choose a type of garden to complement seasonally used spaces—woodland and perennial borders for spring gardens and cutting gardens, summer perennials and annuals for around a swimming pool. Try a back-door herb, kitchen, vegetable, or cutting garden. The closer you are to your gardens, the more you will appreciate them and enjoy working in them. Make sure the sun, shade, soil, water, and drainage are appropriate for your garden plan, but don't be afraid to experiment and try something risky or new.

Planting Seedlings in the Garden

1. Gently tap a seedling to remove from a pot.

2. Push a seedling out of a plastic pack.

3. Plant the seedling at the soil level; leggy tomato plants will root along their stems if planted deeper in soil or on a slant.

4. Firm the soil and water the seedling.

Planting by the Moon—Plant leafy or fruiting vegetables during a waxing moon and root crops during a waning or new moon. The moon will draw up to the light those plants that mature above ground, and keep safe in the dark warmth of the earth those that mature underground. Plant when the moon is in Taurus, Cancer, Virgo, Scorpio, Capricorn, or Pisces. Plow and cultivate when the moon is in Aries, Gemini, Leo, Virgo, Libra, Sagittarius, or Aquarius.

Sowing Seeds Inside
1. Sow two seeds directly into a small pot.

2. Sprinkle seeds on dampened seed potting mix, mist the top, and cover with plastic.

3. Transplant seedlings when they have a set of true leaves besides the initial small seed leaves.

Try sowing peas, beans, carrots, and beets in wide rows.

Companion Planting—Companion planting can cut down on pests later on; for protection and a pleasant variety in the bargain as well, interplant aromatic, insect-repellent flowers, herbs, and vegetables with those less resistant. Aromatics include all the alliums (onions, garlic, chives, scallions, shallots, leeks), marigolds, nasturtiums, basil, dill, thyme, sage, summer savory, rosemary, parsley, artemisia, santolina, tansy, wormwood, and yarrow. Use them where you choose, but use them abundantly.

Plant borage and bee balm to encourage pollination of tomatoes, melons, squashes, etc.

Sowing Seeds in the Garden

1. Sow a line of seeds according to package instructions on depth and spacing.

2. For a trench, sow a wide swath of seeds.

1 All Fool's Day

2

3

4

5

6

7

CHINESE DUCK WITH MIXED
PRESERVES

*Duck roasted with a heady
combination of fruit preserves, and
garlic, ginger, and soy is particularly
flavorful and aromatic. Preserves to
mix include raspberry, blackberry,
black currant, plum, and peach.*

Add 6 minced cloves of garlic and
1 TB chopped fresh ginger to $1\frac{1}{2}$ c
preserves. Prick the skin of a 5 lb
duck, then coat rather than stuff the
duck's cavity with the mixture and
sew shut. Rub the outside of the duck
with soy sauce and sear in a hot wok
with 2 TB oil. Roast the duck in a
preheated 350° oven for 2 hours,
basting it a couple of times. One duck
will feed 2–4 people depending on
their appetites and the rest of the
meal. Two ducks are just as easy to
cook as one.

Duck Puzzle

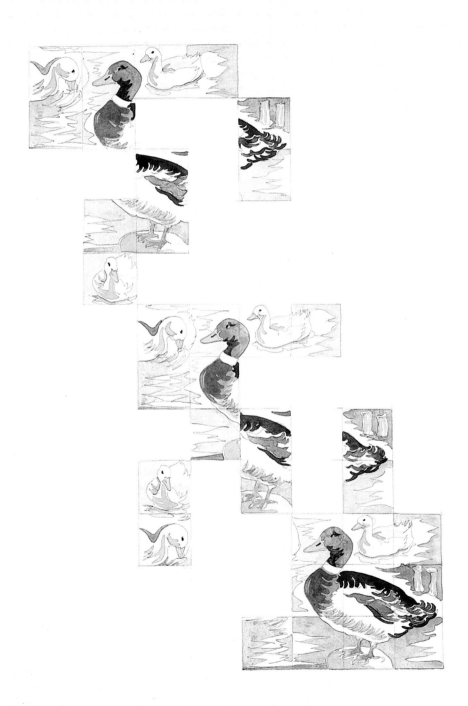

MY FAIRY GODMOTHER'S EASTER EGGS

For special Easter eggs, make patterns using spring flowers and leaves. Gather such flowers as freesias and violets, small leaves, parsley, and blades of grass. Surround a hard-boiled egg with an assortment or just one kind of flower or leaf. Leave some empty space for contrast. Tie the plants with string or rubber bands to hold them tightly to the surface of the egg; these too will make a pattern. Dip the eggs in prepared coloring as usual and the color will fill in around the leaf and flower shapes. For an old-fashioned look, try simmering the eggs in red onion skins for a natural cinnamony color.

9

10

11

12

13

14

Easter Still Life

15

16

17

18

19

20

21

USES FOR VINEGAR

❧ To keep cooked vegetables fresh-looking add 1 TB vinegar to cooking water.

❧ For poached eggs, add 1 TB vinegar to the water to retain the shape of the white.

❧ To prevent eggs from cracking while boiling add 1 TB vinegar to the water.

❧ The addition of vinegar helps to— reduce sweetness in some foods; fluff icing; substitute for a lack of salt, and to marinate or tenderize meat.

❧ Rinse with vinegar to soothe burns, bug bites, and sunburn.

❧ Rinse your hair in cider vinegar to heighten color and shine.

❧ Add 1 c vinegar to bath water for a refreshing body tonic.

❧ Make a cold remedy with 1 TB vinegar and 1 TB honey in a glass of water.

❧ To remove odors from hands wash with soap, then with vinegar, and rub them with salt. Rinse well.

❧ To prevent the color from running in a new cotton garment soak it in 1 part vinegar and 2 parts water for 1 hour before the first washing. (To make hand-painted designs permanent on tee-shirts and other cottons, iron the designs or heat the clothes in the dryer before washing.)

Waterfall with Statues

COVE HOLLOW FARM

REGISTERED HOLSTEINS

HOUSEHOLD TIPS

❧ A cut onion in a large pan of water will absorb the odor of paint in a room.

❧ Clear a room of smoke by swirling a damp towel through the air.

❧ Set out a dish of ammonia and water to cleanse the air in a room or closet.

❧ For Eggs: A fresh egg sinks and an old one floats.

❧ Store eggs large end up to keep the yolk centered.

❧ Prick a small hole in the end of an egg to keep it from cracking while boiling.

❧ When an eggshell cracks during boiling, add a splash of vinegar to seal the crack. Better yet, add it first to prevent cracking.

❧ To prevent the yolks of boiled eggs from turning gray, take care not to overcook them, and cool them quickly after boiling in running cold water.

❧ A hard-boiled egg will spin like a top. A raw egg will wobble.

❧ To separate an egg easily, crack it in your hand and let the egg white slide through your fingers.

23

24

Arbor Day 25

26

27

28

30

NOTES & REMINDERS FOR MAY

Plan for May Day, Mother's Day, and Memorial Day.
Plant lilies and other summer bulbs.
Start herbs from seed outside.
Set out tender vegetables and flowers (tomatoes, basil, squashes, cucumbers, impatiens).
Thin and pinch seedlings in garden.
Plant asparagus roots and begin to harvest rhubarb.
Put houseplants outside.
Make a patio garden in pots or tubs.

Begin cultivation and pest control.
Get summer clothes ready.
Open the pool.
Launch a boat—in the harbor, bay, lake, or pond.
Play tennis or organize a baseball game.
Take breakfast to the beach on a Sunday morning.
Go outside to read or draw.
Go fishing.

MORE NOTES:

Nature Conservancy Sign at the Beach

FLOWER SYMBOLS

Amaryllis — timidity
Anemone — abandonment
Apple — temptation
Bachelor's Button — celibacy
Belladonna — silence
Buttercup — sarcasm
Carnation — capriciousness
Chrysanthemum — optimism
Clematis — artfulness
Clover — fertility
Columbine — cuckoldry
Crocus — attachment
Daffodil — regard
Dahlia — treachery
Daisy — gentleness
Dandelion — coquetry
Dogwood — durability
Edelweiss — immortality
Forget-me-not — true love
Fuchsia — amiability
Gentian — loveliness
Geranium — melancholy
Heather — protection
Hepatica — confidence
Hollyhock — ambition
Honeysuckle — devotion

2

3

4

5

6

7

Plant Shop Facade with Flamingoes

8

9

10

11

12

13

14

MOTHER'S DAY BREAKFAST

A Mother's Day breakfast should be late in the morning—a pretty, leisurely affair to make your mother feel special and a bit spoiled. Choose a special place to serve breakfast: in the garden, on the porch, in a sunny corner, or brought on a tray to be enjoyed in bed. Use flowers, pretty linens and plates, and a touch of imagination; take care over the presentation. Your breakfast or brunch need not be fancy—just indulgent. Consider fresh-squeezed fruit juice, warm muffins or popovers, an egg dish with asparagus, pan-fried trout, or good pastry fresh from the bakery. Do make sure that coffee or tea is the best you can make, and served exactly the way your mother likes it. A small gift, particularly handmade, a day planned around her interests, and dinner out will complete the day. You may find that this sort of special treatment should happen much more often.

Garden Shed with Wicker

Cinnamon & Ginger – May 1985

Lauren Jarrett

FLOWER SYMBOLS

Iris—eloquence
Ivy—marriage
Jonquil—desire
Laurel—success
Lilac—youth
Lily—virginity
Lupine—imagination
Magnolia—beauty
Marigold—jealousy
Morning Glory—farewell
Narcissus—conceit
Nasturtium—conquest
Orchid—magnificence
Peony—bashfulness
Poppy—oblivion
Primrose—inconstancy
Quince—temptation
Rose—charm
Rue—disdain
Snapdragon—desperation
Tulip—dreaminess
Violet—faithfulness
Wisteria—poetry
Woodbine—fraternity
Zinnia—absent friends

16

17

18

19

20

21

Cinnamon and Ginger Iris

22

23

24

HOW TO PAMPER HOUSEGUESTS OR
LEAVE A HOUSE FOR A FRIEND

Make up a pretty bedroom filled with
fresh flowers, magazines, books, a
radio, and, of course, a clock. Supply
the bathroom with necessities,
luxuries, and even more flowers.
Stock the kitchen with fruit and
breakfast treats, whether you make
breakfast for your company or not.
Make sure they know where things
are and how they work. Leave lists of
places to go and things to do and see.
Leave sports equipment, bikes, and
information on beach regulations,
tennis courts, and picnic spots. Leave
emergency phone numbers.

25

26

27

28

Birdhouses for Rent

30

31

NOTES & REMINDERS FOR JUNE

Plan for Father's Day, Flag Day, and
  the Summer Solstice.
Put the rest of the tender vegetables out.
Thin seedlings in the garden.
Pinch back annuals and tomatoes.
Install tomato cages.
Fill window boxes.
Fertilize trees and shrubs.

Deadhead spring shrubs.
Continue to cultivate and control pests.
Put woolen clothes away.
Invite some company for summer weekends.
Paint the trim on the house.
Make an early summer pie.
Sign up for sailing lessons.
Lie in a hammock.

MORE NOTES:

Water Lilies and Frog

1

2

3

ROSE TIPS

A rose bouquet is a special treat which, when cared for, will delight you with its long-lasting blooms. A daily change of water and fresh cuts on the stems will reward you with an extra week of color. Snip the stems at an angle, taking care not to crush the ends, and put them into hot water if they need reviving.

The strength of a rose bush is in its leaves; cut as few as possible—it takes six healthy leaves to produce enough food to make a bloom. Cut above a five-leaf cluster, which is where the next flowering will come.

4

5

6

7

Garden with Animal Statues

CURES FOR POISON IVY

Forget about the myth of using brown laundry soap. The oily resin of poison ivy is best flushed from the skin with lots of rubbing alcohol followed by lots of water, and further cleansed with soap and warm water. If it's too late and the itchy rash is already there, soothe it with the juices of aloe vera, narrow-leafed plantain, jewelweed or touch-me-not, or sweet fern. Apply the juice from the broken or mashed leaves directly to the rash or make a tea with them with which to bathe the area frequently.

9

10

11

12

13

Flag Day 14

Queen Anne's Lace

15

16

17

18

19

20

21

FATHER'S DAY DINNER

For the man who does (or doesn't do) the barbecuing, make a grilled, butterflied leg of lamb and follow with Rhubarb and Strawberry Tart.

GRILLED LEG OF LAMB

Insert slivers of garlic into a butterflied half leg of lamb and marinate it in olive oil, lemon juice, fresh rosemary, and ground pepper. Grill over grayish-white coals, basting the lamb with a sprig of rosemary dipped in the marinade or olive oil. Serve rare to medium rare, along with a summer salad and a good red wine. For 2–4 people, use half a leg of lamb, for 4 or more use a whole leg.

RHUBARB AND STRAWBERRY TART

In a food processor bowl, put 1⅓ c flour, 1 stick butter cut into pieces, 1 tsp salt (less if using salted butter), and 1 tsp sugar. Process 5–10 seconds until the mixture is granular, then add ¼ c ice water and process until a lump of dough forms. Roll out and fit into a 9″ pie pan. Mix ¼ c sugar and 3 TB flour and spread in shell, then add 1 lb rhubarb cut into 1–2″ pieces (about 3 cups), sprinkle with 2 TB sugar, and dot with 1 TB butter. Bake for 1 hour in a preheated 400° oven. While the tart is warm, sprinkle the top with Grand Marnier and arrange sliced strawberries to cover the rhubarb. Serve with cream. Makes one 9″ tart

Sheep Puzzle

ANNIVERSARY GIFT TRADITIONS

1 — paper, plastic, clocks
2 — cotton, china, calico
3 — crystal, glass, leather
4 — linen, silk
5 — wood, silverware
6 — iron, wood
7 — copper, wool
8 — linen, lace, bronze
9 — pottery, leather
10 — tin, aluminum
11 — steel, jewelry
12 — linen, gems
13 — lace, textiles, furs
14 — ivory, crystal, glass
15 — crystal, glass, watches
20 — china, platinum
25 — silver
30 — pearls
35 — coral, jade
40 — ruby
45 — sapphire
50 — gold
55 — emerald
60 — diamond
75 — diamond

23

24

25

26

27

28

Farmhouse Wall

NOTES & REMINDERS FOR JULY

Plan for Independence Day.
Trim herbs and use trimmings for flavoring oils or
   vinegars, or dry them for cooking or making
   sachets.
Raise height of lawn mower.
Side-dress the vegetable garden.
Plan and dig a new plot for next year.
Make a compost pile.
Deadhead annuals.
Cultivate garden; begin pest control.

Plan for weekend guests.
Begin harvesting and preserving of early crops
   (peas, snow peas, beans, broccoli, herbs, etc.).
Go berry picking.
Make a fruit tart.
Organize a croquet or badminton afternoon.
Sit out at night with the stars.
Take a kid to the park.
Make a sand castle.
Make ice cream.

MORE NOTES:

_____

_____

_____

_____

_____

_____

_____

_____

_____

Lauren's Garden

Summer

Summer is the season of beginning bounty and continued chores; it's the time when late planting, maintenance, early harvesting, and preserving all come together in a rush.

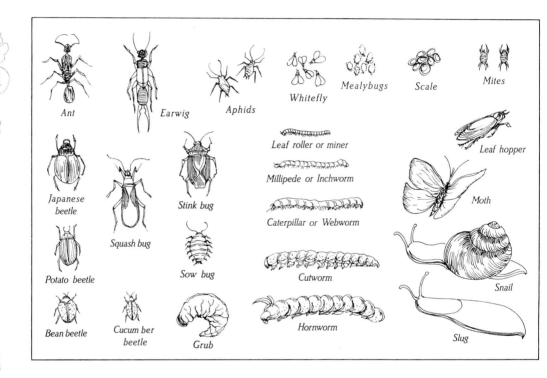

Ant

Earwig

Aphids

Whitefly

Mealybugs

Scale

Mites

Japanese beetle

Squash bug

Stink bug

Leaf roller or miner

Millipede or Inchworm

Caterpillar or Webworm

Leaf hopper

Moth

Potato beetle

Sow bug

Cutworm

Snail

Bean beetle

Cucumber beetle

Grub

Hornworm

Slug

Garden Pests

All gardens, whether rural or city, get pests of one sort or another. Companion plant or arrange aromatics with less resistant plants to help ward off pests. Use a variety of plants to confuse insects; rotate crops to avoid a buildup of a particular plant's worst enemy.

Know your enemy; use the drawings to find out what you've got.

To rid your garden of slugs, sink a cup of beer at ground level to attract and drown them, or set out empty grapefruit halves as "dome" traps.

Protect vegetables from cutworms by placing collars around them set into the ground.

Make an aromatic spray by combining hot peppers, horseradish, tansy, tomato leaves, and pine in a processor or blender. Add a bit of liquid soap and more water to the puréed plant material and spray it on effected plants, particularly on the undersides of the leaves.

Attract birds by feeding them in the fall and winter; they will thank yo by eating millions of insects in the summer, and they add to the pleasu of a garden.

Attack bugs with a spray made from those same bugs; collect an identify the target, buzz a handful in a processor or blender, and strai Dilute with water as much as 8 to 1 and spray the affected plar particularly under the leaves.

To combat Japanese beetles, consider introducing milky spore fung into the ground. Try importing ladybugs or praying mantis for help controlling insects.

Mothproof inside with cedar and herbs (artemesia, lavender, mi santolina, tansy, wormwood, and yarrow).

In the Garden

1. *Thin seedlings sown directly in the garden to provide room for the plants to grow; use the young trimmings in a salad.*

2. *Pinch back small plants to encourage bushy growth.*

3. *Deadhead flowers for continued bloom.*

4. *Stake plants that need support; install tomato cages and trellises or poles for climbers (peas, beans, cucumbers, melons, and squash).*

Summer maintenance in the garden includes sidedressing with fertilizer or compost, watering, spraying to control pests, and cultivating or mulching to control weeds and conserve moisture in the soil. Good mulching materials are pine bark or chips, compost, ground up leaves (not maple), straw, salt hay, and black plastic.

Try a summer salad, soup, garnish, side dish, vinegar, or tea of garden flowers for color, variety, and fun. Borage, calendula, chives, day lily, marigold, nasturtium, rose, and squash blossoms are among the edible flowers in most gardens. Fresh, dried, simmered, or fried—all can be added to your favorite summer recipes.

Pick vegetables at the end of the day when their vitamin content is highest.

Herbs

Use early trimmings from herbs for drying, flavoring oils or vinegars, for herbal teas, or for homemade batches of fines herbes or bouquet garni. Fines herbes is a mixture of parsley, chervil, chives, and tarragon. Bouquet garni is traditionally a combination of bay leaf, parsley, and thyme but can include basil, celery, chervil, rosemary, savory, and tarragon. The herbs are tied in a bunch and usually removed from a dish before serving.

Harvest herbs on a dry, sunny day before they start to fade. Bunch thin stemmed herbs and hang to dry. Spread out thick leaves (comfrey), flowers, berries, or fruits on old screens covered with paper. When the leaves crumble and the berries are hard and shriveled, pack them lightly in jars or tins, and store them in a cool, dark place.

Drying Herbs

1. *Herbs hanging to dry.*

2. *Herbs spread out to dry.*

ICE CREAM

The ice cream cone is a twentieth-century innovation, but in various forms ice cream, frozen ice desserts, and fruit juice over snow have been favorites for centuries. Folks in the north seem to eat more of it, and fancier kinds, than anywhere else. Dish, cone, soda, sundae, simple, fancy, gooped up, or plain—the choice is endless. Try making your own with the hand-cranked type ice cream freezer that my grandfather used, or one of the electric varieties.

MY FAVORITE RASPBERRY OR
STRAWBERRY ICE CREAM
2 c fresh, mashed berries
1 qt heavy cream
1 c sugar
1 TB lemon juice
2 TB pure vanilla extract
½ tsp salt

Mix berries with sugar and let them sit at room temperature for about an hour, then add remaining ingredients and mix well; chill. Chill the ice cream can and dasher for an hour, then fill the can ¾ full with the mixture, and set in the ice cream freezer bucket. Alternate layers of crushed ice and rock salt around the inner canister. It takes about a half hour of steady cranking to get the ice cream about the thickness of mashed potatoes; then put it in the freezer for an hour or two, or as long as you can wait. Be sure to thoroughly clean the ice cream freezer. Makes about 1 quart

2

3

Independence Day 4

5

6

7

8

9

10

KITCHEN TIPS

❦ Peaches, pears, and tomatoes will peel easily after a dip in boiling water.

❦ Remove fruit stains from your hands by washing with lemon juice and salt, and rinsing with water.

❦ A halved potato added to a pot while cooking vegetables will absorb any excess salt.

❦ Try adding sorrel, garlic, or lemon to a recipe as a substitute for salt.

❦ To sweeten the taste of oily fish soak it overnight in the refrigerator in a solution of 3 TB salt and 2 tsp baking soda to 1 gallon of water. Soak the fish for at least six hours, then rinse and pat dry.

11

12

13

14 Bastille Day

Laundry in the Yard

CUT FLOWER TIPS

❦ Most florists include a packet of bloom-extender with cut flowers and arrangements, but for flowers fresh out of the garden or bought from a stand, you can make your own. Combine 1 pint water, 1 pint clear soda, and a few drops of chlorine bleach.

❦ To keep a flower arrangement fresh and smelling sweet add a small piece of charcoal to the water.

❦ Try extending the life of your cut flowers by putting them in the refrigerator during the day if you're not going to be home.

16

17

18

19

20

21

23

24

25

26

27

28

SUMMER SALADS FOR ANY MENU

Garden Salad: salad bowl lettuce, ruby lettuce, arrugula, basil, and chives from the garden

Tomato Salad: marinated with sliced red onions, basil, and mozzarella cheese, drizzled lightly with extra virgin olive oil, or just warm from the garden with a dash of salt & pepper

Dilled Cucumber Salad: with apple cider vinegar

Sugar Snaps and Baby Carrot Salad: serve briefly steamed with a dill vinaigrette

Yellow and Green Bean Salad: in a chunky shallot and walnut dressing

Chunky Beet Salad: tossed with vinegar, a little oil, chopped dill, and salt and pepper

Heartburn Salad: red Bermuda onion, kidney beans, chopped tomatoes, and cracked black pepper in a tart vinaigrette

Chick pea Salad: with peeled red peppers, olives, and Italian parsley

Rice Salad: with artichoke hearts, niçoise olives, and lemon zest

Cracked Wheat Salad: with chopped fresh herbs (including mint) and chives, lemon and oil

Broccoli and New Potato Salad: in a lemon vinaigrette

Fruit Salad: summer berries, sliced peaches, and melon with fresh mint leaves

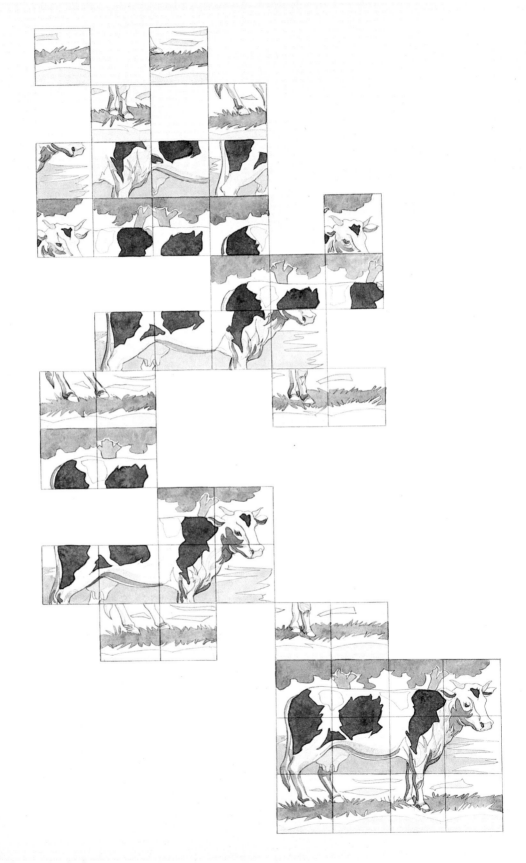

NOTES & REMINDERS FOR AUGUST

Plan for summer weekends and High Summer (August 1).
Lift and divide irises.
Harvest and freeze vegetables and herbs.
Dry flowers for the fall.
Take cuttings of large plants for wintering over.
Pick-your-own if you didn't grow any.
Start thinking about back to school.

Read in the library or go to a museum to beat the heat.
Escape to the mountains or lake.
Have a picnic in the park.
Make lemonade or iced tea for a crowd.
Take the dogs to the beach at night.
Sleep out in the yard or in a screened porch.
Press some wild flowers.

MORE NOTES:

Wild Flowers from a Walk

1 High Summer Day

2

3

4

5

6

7

A HIGH SUMMER BARBECUE

A good barbecue is simple summer fun. Set a careful arrangement of charcoal or aromatic wood, or mix them. Allow 30–45 minutes for whitish-gray coals and spread them out wider than the cooking area. Baste the grill with olive oil to prevent sticking. Cook food on one side, then turn and finish to retain juices. Baste with marinade if you made one.

- Marinate chicken in 2 parts soy sauce and 1 part bourbon with lots of chopped garlic and ginger.
- Marinate steak or swordfish in olive oil and vinegar with extra garlic, lemon, and thyme or rosemary.
- Dampen corn still in the husk and wrap in foil before cooking.
- Try a salad or two from "Summer Salads" (week of July 22–28).
- Remember marshmallows for later.

BRIE DE LA CAMPAGNE

BRIE DE LA CAMPAGNE

PRODUCT OF FRANCE — SOFT RIPENED CHEESE — MADE FROM PASTEURIZED MILK

PICNIC CHECKLIST

Blanket or spread
Baskets
Plates
Napkins
Flatware
Glasses
Cups
Thermos
Cooler
Ice
Serving utensils
Large knife and board
Swiss army knife
Corkscrew and can opener
Matches
Charcoal grill, etc.
Paper towels and foil
Garbage bags (for cleanup)
Flashlight
Shovel and pail (for burying hot
     coals)
Insect repellent
Extra sweat shirts and/or towels
Bags for collecting shells, wild flowers,
     butterflies
Frisbee and paddle set
Surfboards and wet suits for the beach

9

10

11

12

13

14

Brie Label Landscape

15

16

17

18

19

20

21

GARDEN GLUT

When your garden grows faster than you can cook or eat, here are some ways to store up all that good bounty:

- *Zucchini-Corn Mix:* Briefly stir-fry cubed zucchini and raw corn kernels in olive oil and butter, scallions, and seasonings. Cool. Freeze in Ziploc bags and use for camping trip dinners or as a fresh vegetable treat in the winter.
- *All-Year Tomato Base:* Sauté cut-up tomatoes in garlic and olive oil. Strain the juice from the tomatoes and freeze separately for use in sauces and soups.
- *Basil Purée:* Swirl basil, parsley, garlic, and olive oil in a food processor. Seal in Ziploc bags and flatten for freezing. Pieces break off easily for use in winter salad dressings, soups, or to flavor vegetables and fish.
- *Frozen Fruit:* Freeze whole strawberries, raspberries, or blackberries to enjoy in the winter. Wash unbruised fruit, dry, and spread it out on a tray to freeze quickly. Then bag it for future use.

Tractor with Vegetables

BACK TO SCHOOL CHECKLIST

Depending on just where and what school is, remember the following:

Pencils, erasers, sharpener, pens, ruler, notebooks

Drawing pencils and erasers, charcoal, pens and ink, drawing pads

Markers, colored pencils, watercolors

Acrylic or oil paint set, canvas, brushes

Mechanical pencils, protractor, compass set, triangles, scales, rules, squares

Pocket calculator

Dictionary, thesaurus, typewriter, word processor

Microscope

Gym suit, sweat suit, sneakers, gym bag

Book bag, duffle bag, soft luggage set with suit carrier

Laundry bag

Clock, radio, hair dryer, cassette player, stereo, television, VCR

Frisbee, football, tennis racket, bike, skis

If it's an apartment that needs furnishing, forget the list— just empty your house and kitchen, starting with the food processor.

23

24

25

26

27

28

Circus Elephants

30

31

NOTES & REMINDERS FOR SEPTEMBER

Plan for Labor Day and back to school.
Bring houseplants inside, but first check them for
  bugs.
Plant spring bulbs.
Divide day lilies.
Dry flowers.
Plant trees or shrubs.
Make notes on harvest for next year (successes,
  failures, changes, new plans).

Fertilize soil, lawn, and garden.
From Sept. 20–Oct. 31 keep poinsettia and
  Christmas cactus away from light.
Bring woolen clothes out.
Visit some farm stands.
Take a class in something new.
Go antique hunting.
Go camping.

MORE NOTES:

Morning Glories

September

1

LABOR DAY PASTA FOR A CROWD

The idea is simple: have ready all kinds of pasta from fettucine to spirals, from plain to that flavored with tomato, spinach, or beets. Set out bowls of pasta sauces and hot pasta for guests to mix and match.

- Make fresh red tomato and yellow tomato sauces separately to put over multi-colored spirals. Try fresh yellow pepper and red pepper sauces on top for a contrast of color and flavor.
- Mix tuna, capers, and roughly chopped tomatoes or broccoli, cauliflower, and black olives over large pasta shells.
- Toss tomato fettucine with sautéed fresh herbs, garlic, and your favorite mushrooms in olive oil.

2

Round Swamp Farm

8

9

10

11

12

13

14

HERBS AND THEIR USES

Basil (purée in olive oil and freeze) *Uses:* pesto, oils, vinegars, pasta, chicken, fish, soups, salads, stews

Bay Laurel (dry) *Uses:* bouquet garni, fish, soups, stews

Chamomile (dry) *Uses:* tea, potpourri, hair rinse

Chervil (freeze) *Uses:* fines herbes, soups, sauces

Chives (freeze) *Uses:* salads, soups, garnish

Comfrey (dry) *Uses:* medicinal tea, compress, soak

Dill (freeze leaves, dry seeds) *Uses:* seeds for pickles, leaves for salads, soups, stews, fish, chicken

Fennel (freeze leaves, dry seeds) *Uses:* lamb, pork, soups

Garlic (dry) *Uses:* valuable medicinal, soups, salads, chicken, stews, lamb, beef

Lavender (dry) *Uses:* potpourri, sachet, moth bags, dried arrangements

Lemon balm or verbena (dry) *Uses:* tonic tea, bath herb, potpourri

Marjoram (dry) *Uses:* soups, sauces, vegetables, roasts

Mint (dry) *Uses:* tea, fruit, desserts, potpourri

Nasturtium (dry) *Uses:* edible flowers, leaves high in vitamin C

Parsley (freeze) *Uses:* soups, salads, stews, vegetables, garnish, tonic tea, high in vitamins and minerals

Rosemary (dry) *Uses:* soups, lamb, pork, tonic tea, potpourri, hair rinse

Sage (dry or freeze) *Uses:* soups, salads, stuffings, tonic tea

Sorrel (dry or freeze) *Uses:* soups, salads, cooked vegetable

Tarragon (freeze) *Uses:* soups, chicken, fish

Thyme (dry or freeze) *Uses:* bouquet garni, soups, stews, fish, chicken

Dried Herbs and Garlic

September

CAMPING CHECKLIST

Roughing it is more fun if you have along the following:

Packs, tent, sleeping bags, air
    mattresses
Mess kits, stacking nest of pots,
    utensils, camp stove and gas
Saw, matches, fire starter, flashlights,
    water jugs, canteen, candles
Water purification kit, first aid kit, sun
    shower
Toilet articles, shovel, insect repellent,
    pocket knife
Emergency blanket, rain poncho
Extra socks and shoes
Coffee, tea, fruit drink mix, hot
    chocolate mix, sugar, salt, pepper,
    spice kit, olive oil, grated Parmesan
    cheese
Chocolate, mixed nuts, dried fruit,
    hard cheese, salami, canned bacon,
    crackers, fruit, cookies, hot cereal
    mix
Frozen muffins, frozen zucchini and
    corn mix, frozen steak in cooler
A bottle of wine, a bag of brownies,
    food for the dogs if you take them
A book to read, a journal to write in,
    a sketchbook, a camera
. . . and a small flask of good cognac
    to bring out while you sit by the
    fire, watch the stars, or huddle in
    your tent.

16

17

18

19

20

21

Canada Geese with Wind Toys

22

23

24

25

26

27

28

FORCING BUDS ON CHRISTMAS PLANTS

Poinsettias are Mexican wild flowers, grown commercially for Christmas because of their colorful flowering bracts. According to Mexican legend, a small boy knelt in front of a crèche on Christmas Eve with nothing to offer. He prayed and from where he knelt, a beautiful plant, the poinsettia, grew for him to present. To insure blooms at Christmastime, poinsettias must have 9 to 10 hours of light and 14 to 15 hours of complete, undisturbed darkness to simulate the waning light in autumn from September 22 until October 15. Once the buds are set, or if you have purchased a plant in bud or bloom, caring for poinsettias is easy—they only need occasional watering. Various Thanksgiving and Christmas cactus are not as demanding as poinsettias, but they do need shorter days and longer nights (at least 12 hours) to bring on budding and blooming. Take care not to overwater them while they are flowering.

30

NOTES & REMINDERS FOR OCTOBER

Plan for Halloween.
Make a Halloween costume and a harvest figure.
Look for and carve a pumpkin.
Start amaryllis and other bulbs for Thanksgiving.
Dig up tender bulbs.
Fertilize and lime lawn.
Plant trees or shrubs.
Collect holiday wreath material.

Clean up pool, yard, boat.
Put summer clothing away.
Go to a museum and a show.
Organize a football picnic.
Go on a "leafing" weekend.
Pick apples.
Make bread.

MORE NOTES:

Autumn

Whether you cut a branch, pick a fruit, or gather up greens, offer
thanks to the plant spirit that gives you harvest.

Indian summer is the unseasonably warm period after the first frost.

Before the first frost, pull up tomato plants roots and all, and hang them upside down in a cool, dark place.

As well as an apple a day, garlic also keeps the doctor away. Used in salads, soups, oils, vinegars, tinctures, drinks, syrups, and poultices, garlic prevents or cures colds, aids in controlling hypoglycemia, hypertension, and artereosclerosis, lessens asthma and mononucleosis, draws pain from bruises, wounds, or arthritis, quiets, tranquilizes, and is a strong antibiotic, infection fighter, and natural cleanser.

Deep-rooted perennials with tuberous or fibrous roots can be planted in the fall—baby's breath, day lilies, globethistles, hostas, iris, monkshood, peonies, phlox, poppies. Spring bulbs should be planted according to their size (depth) and in groups for a more lush display.

For a spring harvest, plant in the fall. Try a pre-season sowing of lettuce, spinach, peas, parsley, dill, garlic, and maybe kale, chard, radishes, and turnips. Much of what you plant will winter over and surprise you in the spring.

Mulch perennials, trees and shrubs, bulbs, and seeds for overwintering after the ground has frozen.

Set up grow lights inside for winter gardening. Use a light soil mix, provide warm, moist conditions with good circulation, and do not crowd your plants. Try growing lettuce, radishes, carrots, spinach, parsley, dill, chives, thyme, or tomatoes.

Plant a bay tree near your house to protect against lightning.

Plant a tree or shrub in a hole large enough for roots to spread. Enrich the soil and make sure that tree is planted in the ground at the same level it had been at in the pot.

1. Bare rooted—spread the roots out as soil is added.

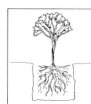

2. Balled in burlap—loosen rope around the ball and cut away any burlap above the ground level.

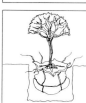

3. Container grown—spread the roots out or cut the larger roots in a few places to prevent them from girdling later on.

4. Stake the tree or shrub, make a well to hold water, soak, and prune back the plant by ⅓ to counter shock and encourage growth.

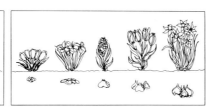

1. A bulb planter is a useful tool when planting bulbs.

2. Plant bulbs at a depth about 3 times their height.

Pruning

Prune newly planted trees and shrubs.
Prune early spring flowering shrubs after flowering.
Prune later flowering shrubs in early spring.
Prune grapes and berry bushes in late winter or early spring.

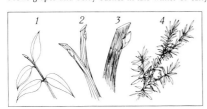

1. Prune a flowering or fruiting stem at a 45° angle just above a bud that faces out so that the new shoot will grow away from the center.
2. Prune deciduous shrub branches at a 45° angle above new buds.

3. Prune tree branches at a 45° angle above an outside dormant bud.
4. Prune the tips of evergreen shrubs and reduce pine candles by ½ to encourage bushy growth.

Wreaths

1. Wire bunches of cones, nuts, berries, shells, etc.

2. Wire and tape bunches of herbs, dried flowers, or greens.

3. Attach bunches to a straw wreath base.

4. Wire loose bunches of greens, flowers, or herbs to a wire frame. Add wired decorations to the completed wreath.

5. Wreath

Holiday wreaths can include: bay laurel, chamomile, cinnamon sticks, dusty miller, pearly everlasting, lavender, marjoram, nutmeg, oregano, rosemary, sage, tansy, thyme, wormwood, frankincense, myrrh, grains, spruce, fir, ash, oak, holly, ivy, pine, juniper, and yew, and anything else that you can wire and add to the wreath.

Dried Herb and Flower Potpourri—
☙ Combine 1 c thyme, 1 c orange mint, 1 c bergamot, 1 c mixed blossoms, ¼ c tarragon, ¼ c rosemary, 1 oz orris root, and 6 drops oil of bergamot.
☙ Combine 2 c lavender, 1 c mint, ½ c thyme, ¼ c rosemary, red geranium, delphinium, bachelor's button petals, and a few drops of oils of lavender, thyme, and bergamot.
☙ Combine 6 c rose petals, 1 c thyme, 1 c rosemary, 1 c marjoram, 1 c lavender, 1 c basil, 6 crushed bay leaves, 1 TB allspice, 1 tsp anise seed, and the dried rind of 1 orange and 1 lemon.

Sachet is simply potpourri tied up in pretty bags, bundles, or pillows.

Pomander balls: stud apples or oranges with log-stemmed cloves. Mix ½ lb mixed ground spices (cinnamon, cloves, ginger, nutmeg) in a large bowl with 2 oz orris root. Turn the balls to cover and leave in the bowl, turning daily until they have dried. To hang the balls, attach ribbons and bows. To renew an old pomander ball, put a drop of clove oil on it and roll it in a bowl of spices, and keep it there for a few days.

Pomander Ball

1

2

3

4

5

6

7

APPLES

Apples	(Flavor)	Eating	Baking
Astrachan	(sweet)	good	good
Baldwin	(mellow)	fair	fair
Cortland	(mild)	excellent	excellent
Red Delicious	(sweet)	excellent	fair
Yellow Delicious	(mild)	good	fair
Empire	(sweet)	excellent	good
Granny Smith	(tart)	good	fair
Gravenstein	(tart)	good	good
Ida Red	(crisp)	good	good
Jonathan	(crisp)	good	good
McIntosh	(crisp)	good	excellent
Macoun	(crisp)	excellent	good
Northern Spy	(crisp)	good	good
RI Greening	(tart)	fair	good
Rome Beauty	(sweet)	good	good
Russet	(tart)	good	good
Winesap	(tart)	excellent	good

Apple Lore
Apples are the sacred fruit of Britain.
Apples remaining on the trees after the
  fruit harvest must be left for the
  elves.

Fruit Bags and Labels

GLEN ORA

MOSS ROSE BRAND

¼ Peck

WICKHAM'S FRUIT FARM
CUTCHOGUE, LONG ISLAND

Orchard Fresh Fruit

½ PECK

Finest Fruit

Local   2 25

CORTLAND   5 LBS.

the choicest of fruit

MY GRANDMOTHER'S SPICE COOKIES

¾ c shortening
1 c sugar
¼ c molasses
1 egg
2 tsp baking soda
2 c flour
½ tsp ginger
½ tsp cloves
1 tsp cinnamon
1 tsp salt

Mix the ingredients well. Form dough into small balls with a spoon and roll them in your hands. Then roll them in sugar and place them on a greased cookie sheet. Bake for 10–15 minutes in a preheated 350° oven. Makes about 5 dozen cookies, depending on how large you make the balls

9

10

11

Columbus Day 12

13

14

Chicken Still Life

16

17

18

PEASANT SOUP

Chop 3 medium onions, 4 cloves garlic, 6 leeks, 3 celery stalks, 4 peeled carrots, and 1 parsnip (optional), and sauté in olive oil. Add salt, pepper, and herbs. Cube 8–10 potatoes and cook in chicken broth and water to cover until done but not mushy. Add vegetables to potatoes and broth, heat through, and adjust seasonings. Serve as is or process to desired smoothness. Try adding 1 c or more of chopped watercress, parsley, arrugula, chives, or spinach either as a garnish or to purée into the soup for a different taste each time. You can also add a little butter or cream to the puréed version if you're feeling decadent. This recipe makes enough to serve 4–6 people for dinner and put 2–3 quarts in the freezer for another time.

19

20

21

1976
Estate Grown
№ 2001

Hargrave Vineyard

North Fork
Long Island   New York

Cabernet Sauvignon

Table Wine Produced & Bottled By Hargrave Vineyard Cutchogue, N.Y.

NARCISSUS

Narcissus blossoms usually last about 10 days, so to enjoy their lovely scent continuously, pot up a few bulbs each week. Their needs are simple: good support (pebbles), water, and light. Put the bulbs on a bed of pebbles, fill in around them with extra pebbles, and add enough water to cover the bottom halves of the bulbs. Water them just to the base of the bulbs thereafter. Narcissus can be grown in full light and will flower in about 4 weeks. Start them in mid-October for Thanksgiving, and continue as desired until spring. Buy fresh bulbs and discard them after forcing.

23

29

30

31

NOTES & REMINDERS FOR NOVEMBER

Plan for Thanksgiving.
Start shopping for the holidays.
Start amaryllis and other bulbs for Christmas.
Mulch the garden.
Store firewood.
Plan ahead for a live Christmas tree—dig a hole
    and cover it with black plastic.
Make wreaths of greens, flowers, herbs, nuts,
    berries, shells, etc.

Reduce houseplant fertilizer to ½ strength.
Get out winter sports equipment.
Make candles, cookies, breads, and kitchen
    presents for the holidays.
Have a nouveau beaujolais party to sample the
    first of the season.
Make a fire to sit and read by.
Play in a leaf pile.

MORE NOTES:

Amagansett Farmer's Market

Celebrate the harvest and join in old customs observing the waning year. At Samhain (witches Sabbath), autumn harvests were used for elaborate feasting before winter set in. The end of the harvest was the symbolic killing of the corn spirit, to be reborn the following spring. Early bonfires and masquerades to appease and ward off spirits and wandering souls turned into today's Halloween customs.

BAKED CREAM OF PUMPKIN SOUP

Cut a lid out of a 4½ lb pumpkin, and scrape out the fibers and seeds. In a slow oven toast about 1 c fresh bread crumbs. Meanwhile sauté 1 c chopped onions in 4 TB butter until soft; add the bread crumbs and cook about 10 minutes. In another skillet, cook 3 slices diced slab bacon until the fat is rendered. Remove from skillet and drain. Stir the bacon, salt, and pepper into the onion mixture, and remove from heat. Then fold in ½ c grated Gruyère and ¼ c grated Parmesan. Spoon this into the pumpkin, add about 1 pint light cream and a little stock, if desired. Cover with pumpkin lid. Bake in a 400° preheated oven for about 1½ hours, or until pumpkin begins to turn a deep russet color; reduce temperature to 350° and continue baking another 20–30 minutes. To serve, ladle out the creamy mixture and scoop out the soft pumpkin flesh. Serves 4 as a main course, or 6 as a starter

Laying Mash and Squash

8

9

10

AMARYLLIS

An amaryllis potted in early November will bloom at Christmas. Choose a pot 2″ larger than the bulb in order to have a 1″ space all around. Line the bottom of the pot with gravel and suspend the bulb as soil is added around the roots. The bulb should be ⅔ out of the ground. One thorough watering is enough until some growth shows. Amaryllis like 4 hours of sunlight and temperatures around 60 degrees at night and 70 degrees during the day. After blooming, the foliage must be allowed to grow during the spring and summer, until it yellows. To begin the cycle anew in the fall, trim the old leaves, clean the bulb of old soil, and repot it in the same pot.

11 Veteran's Day

12

13

14 Sadie Hawkin's Day

Amaryllis

GINGERBREAD DOUGH FOR COOKIES
OR A HOUSE

1 ½ c dark brown sugar
1 egg
2 TB molasses
1 TB corn syrup
2 tsp baking soda in 2 TB hot coffee
4 tsp cinnamon
3 tsp ginger
3 tsp cloves
2 tsp nutmeg
1 c melted butter
4–5 c flour

Mix all ingredients except flour, then
add flour to make a stiff dough. Dust
dough, and roll out directly on
greased and floured cookie sheets. Put
a damp cloth under the cookie sheet
to keep it from moving. For a
gingerbread house, working directly
on the cookie sheets is helpful when
cutting house parts from a pattern.
This way, they will stretch and distort
less, thus making assembly easier later
on. Cut out shapes, reroll trimmings,
and use again. Bake in a preheated
350° oven for 10–15 minutes. After
10 minutes, remove the house pieces,
and check them against the paper
patterns, trim edges where necessary,
and finish baking. Makes enough for
1 small house or 2 dozen gingerbread
men. Or, make a double batch and
hang some of the cookies with ribbon
from a Christmas tree.

16

17

18

19

20

21

Courtyard with Cat

22

23

24

25

26

27

28

ovember

GOOSE WITH FLAVORED WILD RICE
STUFFING

*Cook your goose with this rich
stuffing of wild rice, mushrooms,
walnuts, and prunes.*

Cook 1 c wild rice in 4 c salted
water until almost done. Melt 1 stick
butter and 3 TB olive oil; sauté the
neck, giblets, and liver until done.
Remove. Chop giblets and liver. Sauté
3 finely chopped onions and 3 stalks
finely chopped celery until translucent.
Add 2 c rough-chopped mushrooms
and cook 2 minutes. Season with salt,
pepper, and thyme. Mix with wild
rice, 1 c chopped walnuts, and 1 c
chopped, pitted prunes to form
stuffing, tasting as you go. Prick the
skin of an 8–10 lb goose, and rub
with salt; season the cavity. Fill the
bird loosely with stuffing, and sew the
opening shut. Bake extra stuffing
separately. Roast the goose in a
preheated 400° oven for 1 hour, then
at 350° for 1–1½ hours, or more.
Cook until the thigh juices run
yellowish-pink, not reddish. Baste
occasionally and pour off or suction
off excess fat. Makes 8 servings

Goldenrod and Plum Jar

ORANGEDALE SUNFLOWER

REDLANDS
GOLDEN ROD

L'Imperatrice Plum

30

NOTES & REMINDERS FOR DECEMBER

Plan for the Christmas holidays.

Decorate with wreaths, greenery, herbs and spices, nuts and berries, seasonal plants, flowers, and ribbons.

Stop houseplant fertilizer until February.

Send Christmas cards and packages by December 8th.

Find and check lights and decorations for the tree.

String popcorn and cranberries for the tree.

Make treats for the birds.

Make a gingerbread house.

Donate some toys and gifts to charity.

Make a Christmas list—and make sure you're on it.

Finish holiday shopping.

Fill the house with the scents and sound of the holidays.

Remember to leave out cookies and milk for you-know-who on Christmas Eve.

MORE NOTES:

Two Stumps

1

2

Christmas is coming the goose is
   getting fat
Please put a penny in the old man's
   hat.
If you haven't got a penny,
Then a ha'penny will do.
If you haven't got a ha'penny,
   Then God Bless You.
                    (Mother Goose)

Christmas comes but once a year,
But when it comes it brings good
   cheer.
                    (Mother Goose)

3

4

5

6

7

All Goose Arrangement

GOLDEN GLOW

EMPERORS

foies gras

ROUGIE

CHRISTMAS TIPS

As the winter solstice approaches, follow the old traditions associated with the season. Make a wreath to symbolize continuance, immortality, and the eventual return of spring. Light candles and a yule log (ash or oak) to rekindle the winter sun.

- Candles will burn dripless if refrigerated for several hours before use.
- Candle wicks should be lit once before company arrives; unlit wicks are a sign of inhospitality.
- Rosemary is the herb of welcome; use it in your holiday decorations. Use a sprig of rosemary to stir a wassail bowl of your favorite spiced wine.
- Christmas herbs include ivy, laurel, holly, pine, fir, spruce, yew, cedar, and juniper.
- Holly and mistletoe berries are poisonous; poinsettia leaves are dangerous if eaten.
- Make sure your Christmas tree is secure in its stand, watered frequently, and away from any fire source. Live trees should be brought in just before Christmas and taken outdoors to be planted right after Christmas.

9

10

11

12

13

14

15

16

17

18

19

20

21

CHRISTMAS LORE

A windy Christmas is a sign of good fortune.

A cricket chirping at Christmas brings good luck.

A person born on Christmas Day can see ghosts.

Bells and chimes must be sounded on Christmas Day to frighten away evil spirits.

If the sun shines through the trees at noon on Christmas Day, the next crop will be full.

You will have one lucky month for each cook whose pudding you eat on Christmas Day.

Good luck on Christmas is a "favored young man" who enters the house without a word, throwing grain before him. He tastes all the holiday food and leaves with good wishes for all.

SIMPLE PLEASURES BLACK FOREST
CAKE

One 10″ chocolate genoise cake split
into 3 layers
For frosting:
    1 can sour or sweet cherries
    Kirsch
    4 c heavy cream
    10 oz semi-sweet chocolate
    Sugar (optional)
Reserve 1 c liquid of the cherries; add
2 TB kirsch to the syrup plus ½ c
sugar if using sour cherries. Melt the
chocolate and cool. Whip 2 c of the
cream. First fold a bit of the beaten
cream into the cooled chocolate, then
gently fold the chocolate into the bowl
of cream. Sprinkle first cake layer with
⅓ of the kirsch syrup, spread with ½
of the chocolate whipped cream, and
press ½ of the cherries into the
whipped cream. Repeat steps for the
second layer; cover with 3rd genoise
layer and sprinkle top with remaining
kirsch syrup. Whip remaining 2 c
cream with sugar and kirsch to taste.
Frost cake and decorate with chocolate
curls. Makes 8 servings

23

24

Christmas Day 25

26

27

28

Houses in the Snow

30

31 New Year's Eve

NOTES & REMINDERS FOR JANUARY

Send away for seed catalogues to browse through
  on cold nights.
Put houseplants in east or west windows with no
  fertilizer.

Plan for New Year's Eve.
Make resolutions you can keep.
Start a journal.
Get a new journal.

MORE NOTES: